The Competitive Edge: Balancing Innovation and Equity for the Future

by Joseph Martin Beahm

Copyright © 2024
All rights reserved. No part of this book may be reproduced, distributed, or transmitted in any form or by any means, including photocopying, recording, or other electronic or mechanical methods, without the prior written permission of the author, except in the case of brief quotations embodied in critical reviews and certain other noncommercial uses permitted by copyright law.

Publisher: Self-published via Kindle Direct Publishing
ISBN: 9798303980006
First Edition: December 2024

For inquiries, please contact:
Joseph Martin Beahm
Email: joe@jbeahmdesigns.com
Website: www.jbeahmdesigns.com

To those who dare to imagine a better future—and work tirelessly to create it.

Introduction:
Framing the Paradox of Competition

The Promise of Capitalism

Capitalism, as an economic system, has long been heralded as a driver of human progress. It promises efficiency, innovation, and prosperity through the mechanism of competition. Adam Smith's *The Wealth of Nations* famously illustrated this promise with the metaphor of the "invisible hand," describing how individuals pursuing their self-interest inadvertently benefit society. This vision of self-regulating markets has underpinned economic thought and policy for centuries, shaping the trajectory of industrial and technological development across the globe.

Yet, the history of capitalism reveals a persistent and troubling paradox. While competition fuels growth and innovation, it also creates conditions for consolidation and inequality. Successful firms, by leveraging economies of scale, innovation, or strategic acumen, often grow to dominate their markets. Over time, these dominant players stifle competition, suppress wages, and consolidate wealth and power. Instead of the vibrant, competitive markets envisioned by Smith, capitalism frequently produces oligopolies or monopolies that undermine its foundational principles.

This paradox is not merely a theoretical concern. It has profound implications for the lives of billions of people. Rising income inequality, job precarity, and environmental degradation are symptoms of a system that prioritizes profit over people. These issues are exacerbated by globalization and technological advancements, which, while creating unprecedented opportunities, also deepen the divides between winners and losers in the capitalist system. Furthermore, the unchecked power of monopolies often translates into political influence, further eroding democratic principles and limiting governmental capacity to address systemic inequities. This cascading effect highlights the interconnected nature of capitalism's paradox and its far-reaching consequences.

Historically, capitalism emerged from the ashes of mercantilism, where economic policies centered on state control of trade and colonial expansion. The transition to free markets in the 18th century was revolutionary, driven by Enlightenment ideals of individual liberty and economic freedom. Smith's vision was not an endorsement of greed but a call for balance—a market system grounded in fair play and minimal interference from entrenched powers. However, the very forces that dismantled mercantilist monopolies gave rise to new concentrations of power in the industrial age, setting the stage for capitalism's recurring paradox.

Why This Book Matters

The paradox of capitalism—its capacity to innovate and its tendency to consolidate—is the defining economic challenge of our time. From the industrial monopolies of the Gilded Age to the digital monopolies of the 21st century, this dynamic has shaped the trajectory of global economies. Addressing it requires a nuanced understanding of how competition operates, both in theory and in practice.

This book seeks to explore capitalism's paradox through a multidisciplinary lens, integrating insights from economics, history, sociology, and political science. By examining the evolution of competition—its theoretical foundations, historical manifestations, and modern challenges—we aim to uncover pathways for mitigating its destructive tendencies while preserving its capacity for innovation.

This work is not a call to abandon capitalism but to rethink and reform it. Markets can be engines of progress, but only when structured to balance competition with equity, innovation with sustainability, and profit with societal well-being. Achieving this balance is essential for addressing the pressing challenges of our era, from climate change to systemic inequality. This task is further complicated by the rapid pace of technological innovation, which continuously reshapes market dynamics and accelerates the impacts of these challenges.

Moreover, this book addresses a global audience. While the paradox of capitalism manifests universally, its impact varies across regions. In developed economies, the consolidation of wealth and power often leads to stagnant wages and political polarization. In developing economies, the effects are different but equally severe: exploitative labor practices, resource extraction, and limited access to technological advancements.

Understanding these distinctions is critical for designing equitable and effective solutions.

The Stakes

The stakes of addressing capitalism's paradox are immense. Consider the rise of Big Tech, where firms like Google, Amazon, and Facebook dominate their respective markets. These companies drive technological advancement and deliver unparalleled convenience to consumers. Yet, their dominance also raises critical concerns about market fairness, data privacy, and the concentration of economic power. Similarly, the gig economy—hailed as a flexible alternative to traditional employment—has created precarious working conditions for millions, undermining labor protections and deepening economic insecurity. The power imbalance between platforms and workers exemplifies how competition can entrench inequities rather than resolve them.

Beyond the economic sphere, capitalism's contradictions spill into the social and environmental realms. Climate change, arguably the greatest existential threat of our time, is driven by a system that prioritizes growth at any cost. The relentless pursuit of profit has led to resource depletion, biodiversity loss, and rising carbon emissions. Addressing these challenges requires a fundamental rethinking of how markets operate and how they can be aligned with long-term sustainability. Additionally, the global nature of these issues demands coordinated action across borders, highlighting the limitations of purely national approaches to reform.

Consider the agricultural industry, where monopolistic control over seeds and chemicals by firms like Bayer (formerly Monsanto) has marginalized small farmers and stifled biodiversity. Similarly, in healthcare, market concentration has driven up costs while limiting access to life-saving medications. These examples demonstrate that capitalism's paradox is not confined to a single sector but permeates the fabric of global markets, affecting essential goods and services that shape everyday life.

This book is guided by three central questions:

1. How has competition evolved over time to produce consolidation and inequality across industries?
2. What historical and theoretical insights can illuminate capitalism's inherent contradictions?
3. How can markets be reimagined to balance innovation with equity and sustainability?

These questions are not isolated inquiries but interconnected threads that weave through the narrative of capitalism's evolution. They seek to uncover the structural forces that shape markets and the potential pathways for systemic reform.

To address these questions, the book is organized into five parts:

1. **Theoretical Foundations:** This section examines competing visions of competition as articulated by Adam Smith, Karl Marx, and Joseph Schumpeter, alongside insights from modern behavioral economics. These perspectives provide a foundation for understanding capitalism's paradox and its manifestations across different historical and industrial contexts.

2. **Historical Trajectories:** From the monopolistic trusts of the Gilded Age to the labor protections of the New Deal and the deregulation of the neoliberal era, this section traces the historical evolution of competition. It emphasizes the cyclical nature of reform and regression within capitalist systems.

3. **Modern Challenges:** This section analyzes contemporary issues, including the dominance of Big Tech, the precarity of the gig economy, and the global nature of modern markets. It explores how technological advancements amplify both the benefits and pitfalls of competition.

4. **Comparative Frameworks:** By exploring international approaches to competition, labor, and antitrust—including those

of the European Union, China, and emerging economies—this section highlights alternative models for structuring markets. It considers how cultural, political, and economic differences shape regulatory strategies and outcomes.

5. **Policy Solutions:** The final section proposes systemic reforms to address capitalism's contradictions, emphasizing the need for policies that align markets with societal and environmental goals. It focuses on practical solutions that balance innovation with equity and sustainability.

A Journey Through Contradiction

This book is not an argument against capitalism but a call to engage with its complexities. By understanding the mechanisms of competition and its dual nature as both a driver of progress and a source of inequality, we can begin to imagine alternative futures. This journey is both analytical and aspirational, seeking to illuminate pathways for creating a more inclusive and sustainable economic system.

The first step in this journey is to delve into the theoretical foundations of competition, exploring the insights of Smith, Marx, Schumpeter, and others. Their ideas continue to shape our understanding of markets, offering valuable perspectives on the paradoxes that define capitalism today. Let us begin.

Chapter 1:
Competing Visions of Competition

The Invisible Hand and the Promise of Competition

Adam Smith's *The Wealth of Nations* (1776) remains one of the most influential texts in economic thought. Smith envisioned markets as self-regulating systems where competition ensures efficiency, innovation, and societal prosperity. For Smith, competition incentivizes producers to improve their goods and services, benefiting consumers while driving economic growth. His theory emphasized the productive potential of individual ambition and the ways in which decentralized decision-making could lead to aggregate benefits.

However, Smith's vision presupposes ideal conditions: numerous competitors, informed consumers, and minimal power imbalances. In practice, markets deviate from these conditions. Firms that achieve scale gain structural advantages, enabling them to dominate competitors and consolidate power. Over time, this dynamic stifles the very competition that Smith celebrated, creating monopolies and reducing consumer choice. This tension between the theoretical ideal and practical realities sets the stage for the paradoxical outcomes of capitalism.

Smith's optimism also underestimated the role of human behavior in markets. Modern behavioral economics highlights how irrational decision-making, asymmetric information, and herd behavior undermine the self-regulating dynamics Smith envisioned. As a result, markets often fail to deliver equitable outcomes, requiring interventions to restore balance. This need for intervention marks a significant divergence from Smith's ideal, where the invisible hand operates without external interference. Furthermore, Smith's framework does not fully account for the systemic advantages that certain firms gain through technological innovation, regulatory capture, or network effects, all of which increasingly define modern markets.

Marx's Critique: Capitalism's Drive Toward Monopolies

Karl Marx, writing in *Das Kapital* (1867), offered a starkly different perspective on competition. Marx argued that competition among capitalists inevitably leads to consolidation, as larger firms outcompete and absorb smaller rivals. This process, which Marx termed "the concentration of capital," creates economic systems dominated by a few powerful entities. For Marx, this dynamic was not an aberration but an inherent feature of capitalism.

Marx's critique highlights the exploitative nature of this dynamic. As firms consolidate, they gain greater control over labor markets, suppressing wages and working conditions. The result is a system where wealth and power are concentrated in the hands of a few, exacerbating inequality and economic instability. While Marx's analysis was rooted in the industrial capitalism of the 19th century, his insights remain relevant in today's economy, where tech giants and financial institutions wield unprecedented power. The dominance of firms like Amazon and Google exemplifies Marx's prediction of capital concentration, as these companies leverage data, scale, and control over infrastructure to consolidate their market positions.

Marx also emphasized the cyclical crises inherent in capitalist systems. He argued that competition drives overproduction, leading to economic downturns that disproportionately harm workers while enabling dominant firms to consolidate further. These cycles of boom-and-bust underscore the fragility of market systems and their tendency to prioritize profit over societal well-being. Additionally, Marx noted the global implications of capital concentration, as multinational corporations extend their reach into developing economies, often exacerbating existing inequalities.

Schumpeter's Creative Destruction: Innovation Through Disruption

Joseph Schumpeter, in *Capitalism, Socialism, and Democracy* (1942), introduced the concept of "creative destruction." Schumpeter viewed competition as an inherently dynamic process, characterized by cycles of disruption and renewal. He argued that monopolistic firms, while often criticized, can drive innovation by investing in research and development. For Schumpeter, the temporary dominance of these firms was a necessary condition for progress.

However, Schumpeter's optimism assumes that monopolies are temporary and subject to eventual disruption. Dominant firms often use their market power to entrench their positions, suppressing potential competitors through acquisitions, lobbying, and other anti-competitive practices. This tension—between innovation and entrenchment—illustrates the complexities of competition in modern markets.

Schumpeter's theory also raises important questions about the role of policy in fostering innovation. If monopolistic dominance is a precondition for innovation, should policymakers tolerate consolidation to promote technological advancement? Or should they prioritize competition, even at the risk of slowing innovation? These questions remain central to debates about antitrust regulation and industrial policy. Moreover, Schumpeter's framework invites scrutiny of how innovation itself is defined: is it measured solely by technological advancement, or does it encompass broader societal benefits such as equity and sustainability?

Behavioral Economics: Why Consumers Reinforce Monopolies

Behavioral economics challenges the assumption of rational consumer behavior. Instead of seeking competitive alternatives, consumers often prioritize convenience, familiarity, or brand loyalty. This tendency reinforces monopolistic dominance, as seen in the rise of platforms like Amazon and Google.

Amazon, for instance, benefits from network effects: its value increases as more consumers and sellers join its ecosystem. These dynamics create a feedback loop, where dominance begets further dominance. Similarly, Google's control over search and advertising markets stems from its ability to collect and leverage vast amounts of user data, making it difficult for competitors to challenge its position. These dynamics are not limited to technology; industries such as healthcare and finance exhibit similar patterns, where convenience and trust create barriers to competition.

Behavioral economics also highlights the role of cognitive biases in market dynamics. For example, consumers often overvalue short-term benefits, such as low prices or convenience, while underestimating the long-term consequences of monopolistic power. This myopia enables dominant firms to entrench their positions, even as their practices undermine competition. The psychology of choice overload further exacerbates this issue, as consumers default to familiar brands or platforms when faced with overwhelming options.

Reconciling Smith and Marx: The Paradox of Competition

Smith and Marx represent opposing views of competition, yet their ideas converge in significant ways. Smith's optimism about market dynamics contrasts with Marx's critique of their consequences, but both acknowledge the dual nature of competition: it drives progress while creating conditions for consolidation and inequality. Schumpeter's emphasis on creative destruction adds another layer to this analysis, highlighting the cyclical nature of capitalist markets.

This paradox defines capitalism's historical trajectory and modern challenges. Understanding it is essential for navigating the complexities of contemporary markets, where competition continues to shape economic, social, and political systems. The global economy further complicates this paradox, as multinational corporations operate across jurisdictions with varying regulations, often exploiting inconsistencies to entrench their power.

Looking Ahead: Theoretical Foundations in Practice

The theories of Smith, Marx, and Schumpeter provide a foundation for understanding capitalism's paradox, but their implications extend far beyond abstract debates. In the next chapter, we explore how these ideas have played out in practice, tracing the historical evolution of competition from the Gilded Age to the neoliberal era. This journey reveals the enduring relevance of their insights and the ways in which they can inform efforts to create more equitable and dynamic markets. By grounding these theoretical frameworks in historical and contemporary examples, we can better understand the tools and strategies needed to address capitalism's paradox in the 21st century.

Chapter 2: The Gilded Age and Industrial Monopolies

The Gilded Age, spanning the late 19th and early 20th centuries, was a time of extraordinary transformation in American economic and social life. In the wake of the Civil War, the United States underwent an industrial revolution that reshaped its cities, industries, and national identity. Railroads stretched across the continent, steel and oil became the cornerstones of modern industry, and new technologies revolutionized production. This period of explosive growth created an era of unprecedented wealth and innovation, yet it also gave rise to profound disparities in power, resources, and opportunity.

At the heart of this transformation lay a central paradox: the very forces that drove industrial progress—efficiency, innovation, and competition—also laid the groundwork for monopolistic consolidation and societal inequality. As railroads connected the country, facilitating commerce and movement, they also became tools for economic dominance. Steel turned America into a modern industrial giant, yet its production demanded brutal sacrifices from laborers. Oil fueled new industries and possibilities, but its markets were dominated by a single, colossal entity. The Gilded Age, in its dazzling extremes, revealed the dual nature of capitalism: a system capable of lifting nations to new heights while simultaneously entrenching power in the hands of the few.

This chapter explores the driving forces behind the Gilded Age's economic landscape, focusing on the rise of industrial monopolies and the individuals who controlled them. Figures like John D. Rockefeller, Andrew Carnegie, and J.P. Morgan embodied both the promise and the peril of unrestrained capitalism. Their enterprises shaped entire industries, yet their success came at significant social cost. As the era progressed, public resistance to corporate domination and labor exploitation began to take hold, laying the foundations for reform in the years to come.

The industrial giants of the Gilded Age did not simply succeed within existing markets—they created markets, controlled them, and reshaped the economy in their image. John D. Rockefeller's Standard Oil Company provides perhaps the clearest example of this transformation. Rockefeller achieved dominance through a combination of innovation and ruthless strategy. Vertical integration allowed Standard Oil to control every stage of production, from drilling and refining to transportation and distribution. Simultaneously, Rockefeller cut secret deals with railroads, secured preferential rates, and leveraged predatory pricing to undercut competitors, driving many out of business. By the 1880s, Standard Oil controlled more than 90% of the U.S. oil market, achieving a monopoly unmatched in scale. While Rockefeller's efficiency and cost-cutting innovations benefited consumers in the short term, they also underscored the dangers of concentrated economic power. The oil market ceased to be competitive, and wealth flowed upward, solidifying Rockefeller's dominance.

Rockefeller's tactics find echoes in the modern digital age. Companies like Amazon have leveraged vertical integration and preferential partnerships to dominate e-commerce, consolidating their grip on distribution networks while undercutting smaller retailers. Just as Standard Oil reshaped the oil market, Amazon has redefined the concept of convenience and access, often at the expense of smaller competitors and local economies. The parallels remind us that while the industries may change, the patterns of consolidation remain strikingly consistent. These modern monopolies, fueled by algorithms and data, evoke the same concerns about fairness, competition, and economic dependence that defined Rockefeller's reign.

Andrew Carnegie's rise in the steel industry followed a similar path of relentless control and innovation. Carnegie revolutionized steel production by embracing the Bessemer process, a breakthrough that dramatically reduced production costs and made steel the backbone of American infrastructure. His empire, built through vertical integration, encompassed everything from raw material extraction to the railroads that delivered steel to customers. However, Carnegie's efficiency was achieved at the cost of his workforce. Men toiled for 12-hour shifts in suffocating heat, surrounded by molten steel, where even a moment's mistake could mean disfigurement or death. The infamous Homestead Strike of 1892 remains a defining moment of labor resistance, as steelworkers protested against low wages and dangerous working conditions. The strike descended into violence, leaving a scar on Carnegie's legacy and revealing the enormous divide between industrial capital and labor. Carnegie's later philanthropy—his funding of libraries, universities, and cultural institutions—cannot erase the exploitation that built his empire, but it does illustrate the complexity of his legacy.

J.P. Morgan wielded his influence not in steel or oil but in the abstract, yet immensely powerful, realm of finance. Morgan acted as a stabilizer of capitalism, mobilizing capital and orchestrating mergers that created corporate giants like U.S. Steel, America's first billion-dollar corporation. His role during the Panic of 1907, when he singlehandedly rallied financiers to prevent an economic collapse, demonstrated both the necessity and the danger of his power. While Morgan's interventions revealed his ability to impose order on financial chaos, they also exposed a troubling dependency: the American economy had become reliant on the decisions of a single individual. Much like today's financial conglomerates—JPMorgan Chase or BlackRock—Morgan's dominance raised questions about accountability, transparency, and the balance of power between private capital and public governance.

The industrial titans of the Gilded Age reshaped the economic landscape, but their dominance also provoked a growing backlash. Public sentiment began to shift as the consequences of unchecked corporate power became impossible to ignore. Journalists like Ida Tarbell played a critical role in exposing the unethical practices of monopolistic firms. Tarbell's investigative reporting on Standard Oil laid bare Rockefeller's underhanded tactics, galvanizing public opinion and lending momentum to calls for reform. Her work illustrated the power of the press to hold corporations accountable, a role that remains vital in today's scrutiny of tech monopolies and financial giants.

For workers, the Gilded Age was a time of struggle and resistance. Long hours, meager wages, and hazardous working conditions defined the industrial labor experience. The rise of labor unions, including the Knights of Labor and the American Federation of Labor (AFL), reflected workers' growing determination to fight for better treatment. Strikes became powerful symbols of resistance, though they were often met with violent suppression. The Pullman Strike of 1894, which saw federal troops deployed against striking railway workers, underscored the immense power industrialists held over both their workers and the political system. Yet these movements planted the seeds of change, laying the groundwork for labor protections that would emerge in the Progressive Era.

The Sherman Antitrust Act of 1890 represented the federal government's first major effort to regulate monopolistic practices. Though its language was vague and enforcement inconsistent, the Act signaled a recognition that unrestrained corporate power posed a threat to competition and fairness. Judicial interpretations at the time, however, often favored business interests, weakening the Act's immediate impact. It was the beginning of a broader movement toward reform—one that would gain momentum in the Progressive Era, as leaders sought to strike a balance between innovation and equity.

The Gilded Age remains a defining period in American economic history, illustrating both the extraordinary potential and the inherent risks of capitalism. The innovations of Rockefeller, Carnegie, and Morgan laid the groundwork for modern industries, yet their dominance revealed the dangers of unregulated markets. The era's legacy is one of contradiction: progress and exploitation, growth and inequality, opportunity and exclusion.

As the 20th century dawned, the call for reform grew louder. The Progressive Era would bring new policies and new ideas to bear on the challenges of monopolistic power and economic inequality. Yet the tensions of the Gilded Age—between innovation and consolidation, between progress and fairness—persist to this day. Modern giants in technology, finance, and commerce evoke the same questions of power, equity, and accountability that defined the era of Rockefeller, Carnegie, and Morgan. By understanding the Gilded Age, we gain a clearer lens through which to examine our present moment, and the choices we must make to shape a more balanced and equitable future.

Chapter 3: The Progressive Era and New Deal Reforms

The Progressive Era, emerging in the early 20th century, represented a critical response to the excesses of the Gilded Age. The unrestrained industrial growth and monopolistic dominance that characterized the late 19th century had left deep scars on American society—concentrating wealth in the hands of a few while fostering widespread inequality and labor exploitation. As the grip of industrial titans tightened, the need for reform became undeniable, setting the stage for a new era of economic and social intervention. Where the late 19th century was defined by unchecked industrial power, monopolistic dominance, and deep social inequalities, the Progressive Era marked the beginning of meaningful reform. A diverse coalition of reformers—politicians, journalists, labor organizers, and everyday citizens—sought to challenge the concentrated power of industrialists and restore fairness to the economy.

During this time, the federal government took its first significant steps toward regulating markets, curbing monopolies, and addressing the labor exploitation that had come to define industrial capitalism. The Progressive Era, while imperfect and fraught with limitations, was pivotal in reasserting the role of government as a counterbalance to corporate power. It laid the foundation for many of the economic policies that would later emerge under Franklin D. Roosevelt's New Deal, signaling a shift toward greater regulation and accountability in the American economy.

The Rise of Antitrust Laws

The passage of the Sherman Antitrust Act in 1890 marked a watershed moment in American economic history. For the first time, the federal government acknowledged the dangers of monopolistic consolidation and sought to intervene. The Act declared illegal "every contract, combination in the form of trust or otherwise, or conspiracy, in restraint of trade or commerce." However, its vague language and uneven enforcement limited its effectiveness during the Gilded Age. Industrial giants like Standard Oil and U.S. Steel remained largely unchallenged in their dominance.

It was not until the Progressive Era that the Sherman Act was enforced with greater vigor. The administration of President Theodore Roosevelt ushered in a new era of antitrust action. Roosevelt, often referred to as the "Trust Buster," believed that unchecked corporate power threatened democracy and economic fairness. Under his leadership, the federal government filed suits against monopolistic entities, most notably the 1904 case against Northern Securities Company, a massive railroad trust controlled by J.P. Morgan. The Supreme Court's decision to dissolve

Northern Securities set a powerful precedent, demonstrating that even the most formidable industrialists were not above the law.

The momentum continued with the passage of the Clayton Antitrust Act in 1914, which strengthened the Sherman Act by explicitly prohibiting practices like price discrimination, interlocking directorates, and mergers that substantially lessened competition. That same year, the establishment of the Federal Trade Commission (FTC) provided a regulatory body dedicated to monitoring and preventing unfair business practices. These reforms reflected a growing consensus that competitive markets required active oversight, rather than passive reliance on Smith's invisible hand.

Labor Reforms and Worker Protections

While antitrust laws sought to address corporate dominance, the plight of industrial workers became a central focus of Progressive Era reforms. The harsh conditions that characterized factory work during the Gilded Age—long hours, low wages, and unsafe environments—sparked growing calls for labor protections. The Triangle Shirtwaist Factory fire of 1911, in which 146 garment workers perished due to locked exits and unsafe conditions, became a tragic symbol of the need for reform. The fire sparked widespread public outrage, with mass protests and funerals drawing thousands of mourners. Journalists and labor organizers seized on the tragedy to expose the callousness of industrial practices, galvanizing momentum for workplace safety laws and labor protections that had long been ignored.

Labor unions played a critical role in this movement. Organizations like the Industrial Workers of the World (IWW) and the American Federation of Labor (AFL) fought for workers' rights through strikes, protests, and collective bargaining. Though these efforts were often met with fierce resistance from employers and government forces, they brought national attention to the urgent need for workplace protections.

Progressive politicians responded with landmark legislation that sought to improve the lives of workers. States began to pass laws limiting child labor, regulating working hours, and mandating safer workplace conditions. The Keating-Owen Act of 1916, though later overturned, represented a federal attempt to restrict child labor by prohibiting the interstate sale of goods produced by underage workers. These reforms marked the first steps toward the labor protections that would become more robust under the New Deal.

The New Deal: Government as Economic Stabilizer

The reforms of the Progressive Era laid the groundwork for Franklin D. Roosevelt's New Deal, a sweeping response to the economic devastation of the Great Depression. By the 1930s, the failures of unregulated capitalism had become undeniable. The stock market crash of 1929 and the subsequent economic collapse revealed the fragility of a system that prioritized corporate profits over economic stability and fairness. Roosevelt's New Deal marked a decisive shift in the role of government, transforming it from a distant arbiter into an active participant in economic life.

The New Deal introduced a range of policies designed to stabilize the economy, regulate markets, and protect workers. The Glass-Steagall Act of 1933 separated commercial and investment banking, curbing risky financial practices that had contributed to the crash. In the years immediately following its passage, the Act fundamentally reshaped the financial industry by reducing conflicts of interest and preventing banks from engaging in speculative investments that had destabilized the economy. Commercial banks focused on traditional lending and deposit-taking, while investment banks specialized in securities trading and underwriting. This separation restored public confidence in the banking system, contributed to financial stability, and remained a cornerstone of economic regulation for decades until its eventual repeal in the late 20th century. The creation of the Securities and Exchange Commission (SEC) provided oversight of financial markets, ensuring transparency and accountability.

For workers, the New Deal represented a turning point. The National Industrial Recovery Act (NIRA) of 1933 sought to boost wages, stabilize prices, and improve labor conditions through industry codes. Though the NIRA was struck down by the Supreme Court, its principles lived on in subsequent legislation, most notably the Wagner Act of 1935. The Wagner Act guaranteed workers the right to unionize and engage in collective bargaining, marking a historic victory for organized labor.

The Social Security Act of 1935 further solidified the New Deal's legacy, establishing a safety net for the most vulnerable members of society. By introducing unemployment insurance, old-age pensions, and aid for dependent children, the Act reflected a broader commitment to economic equity and social welfare.

Case Studies: Breaking Up Monopolies and Regulating Industries

The Progressive Era and New Deal reforms were not merely theoretical shifts—they produced tangible results in curbing corporate excesses and protecting public interests. One of the most significant examples was the breakup of Standard Oil in 1911. Following years of litigation, the Supreme Court ruled that Standard Oil's dominance violated the Sherman Antitrust Act. The company was dismantled into 34 smaller entities, including what would become Exxon and Mobil. While this breakup did not end corporate dominance entirely, it demonstrated the government's willingness to confront monopolistic power.

Similarly, New Deal programs like the Tennessee Valley Authority (TVA) and the Rural Electrification Administration transformed entire industries by providing public alternatives to private monopolies. The TVA not only brought electricity to impoverished regions but also spurred industrial development, improved agricultural productivity, and laid the groundwork for regional economic growth that persisted for decades. Similarly, rural electrification programs expanded infrastructure to areas long neglected by private utilities, fostering innovation and economic opportunity that would shape rural communities well into the 20th century. The TVA brought electricity, infrastructure, and economic development to impoverished regions, challenging the profit-driven priorities of private utility companies.

The Role of Government in Balancing Markets

The Progressive Era and New Deal represented two pivotal moments when the government intervened to correct capitalism's excesses and inequities. While the Progressive Era focused on antitrust enforcement and labor reforms, the New Deal expanded the scope of government to include economic stabilization and social welfare. Together, these reforms established a precedent for active governance as a means of balancing competition, protecting workers, and promoting equity.

Yet these efforts were not without limitations. Both eras grappled with resistance from powerful corporate interests, judicial opposition, and the complexities of implementing lasting change. Moreover, the benefits of these reforms were often unevenly distributed, particularly among marginalized communities, who faced systemic barriers to economic opportunity.

As we look to the future, the lessons of the Progressive Era and the New Deal remain profoundly relevant. They remind us that capitalism, left unchecked, tends toward consolidation and inequality—but that with thoughtful intervention, it can be reformed to serve broader societal goals. The question of how to balance innovation with fairness, and growth with equity, remains central to the ongoing evolution of our economic systems. Can a modern economy truly thrive if unchecked consolidation and inequality persist, or must we learn from history's reforms to find a more sustainable path forward? These challenges will only deepen as we confront the rise of new monopolies, shifting labor dynamics, and the global implications of capitalism's contradictions.

Chapter 4:
Neoliberalism and Globalization

The mid-to-late 20th century marked a new phase in the evolution of capitalism, defined by two interrelated forces: the rise of neoliberal economic policies and the acceleration of globalization. Emerging from the aftermath of the Great Depression and World War II, the global economy experienced unprecedented expansion. Governments, empowered by the lessons of the Progressive Era and New Deal, adopted regulatory frameworks to stabilize markets and promote social welfare. However, by the 1970s, shifting economic realities, political ideologies, and technological advancements led to a dramatic transformation. The resulting embrace of neoliberalism—characterized by deregulation, privatization, and market liberalization—reshaped economies around the world. Coupled with globalization, this shift created new opportunities for growth while intensifying inequality and destabilizing labor markets.

This chapter explores the origins, principles, and consequences of neoliberalism and globalization. From the policies of Milton Friedman and Friedrich Hayek to the economic revolutions of Reagan and

Thatcher, neoliberalism promised to unleash innovation and economic freedom. At the same time, globalization connected economies across borders, facilitating trade, investment, and technological exchange. Yet, as markets opened and regulations receded, power consolidated in multinational corporations, labor precarity deepened, and the divide between winners and losers became more pronounced. By examining these forces, we can better understand the challenges they pose to equitable competition and sustainable progress.

The Rise of Neoliberalism: Ideology and Policy

Neoliberalism arose in response to the perceived failures of post-war economic systems. By the 1970s, stagflation—a combination of stagnant economic growth and rising inflation—had undermined confidence in Keynesian economic policies, which emphasized government intervention and demand-side management. In this climate of economic uncertainty, economists like Milton Friedman and Friedrich Hayek gained prominence, advocating for a return to free-market principles. They argued that government regulation, welfare programs, and high taxation stifled individual freedom, economic efficiency, and innovation.

Friedman, a leading figure in the Chicago School of Economics, championed monetarism—the belief that controlling the money supply was the key to managing inflation. In his influential book *Capitalism and Freedom* (1962), Friedman outlined a vision of limited government, deregulated markets, and privatization of public services. Similarly, Hayek's *The Road to Serfdom* (1944) warned of the dangers of centralized planning, arguing that economic freedom was inseparable from political freedom. Together, their ideas laid the intellectual foundation for neoliberalism.

The political implementation of neoliberalism began in earnest during the 1980s under the leadership of U.S. President Ronald Reagan and U.K. Prime Minister Margaret Thatcher. Reagan's policies, often referred to as "Reaganomics," emphasized tax cuts, deregulation, and reductions in government spending. By lowering corporate taxes and dismantling regulations, Reagan sought to stimulate economic growth and unleash the power of private enterprise. Thatcher pursued a similar agenda in the United Kingdom, privatizing state-owned industries, weakening trade unions, and championing free-market reforms. Both leaders framed their policies as necessary corrections to years of economic stagnation and government overreach.

The neoliberal agenda soon spread globally through institutions like the International Monetary Fund (IMF) and the World Bank. Developing countries, facing debt crises and economic instability, were encouraged—or compelled—to adopt structural adjustment programs (SAPs). These programs prioritized fiscal austerity, trade liberalization, and privatization as conditions for receiving financial aid. While proponents argued that these reforms would integrate developing economies into global markets, critics contended that they deepened poverty, weakened public institutions, and exacerbated inequality.

Globalization: Opportunities and Inequalities

Globalization accelerated alongside neoliberal reforms, driven by technological advancements, trade liberalization, and the rise of multinational corporations. Innovations in transportation and communication—such as container shipping, the internet, and telecommunications—reduced the costs of global trade and connected markets across continents. Countries embraced free trade agreements, lowering tariffs and barriers to the movement of goods, services, and capital.

The establishment of organizations like the World Trade Organization (WTO) in 1995 formalized the rules of global commerce, promoting the vision of a borderless economy. For many countries, globalization brought economic opportunities, technological progress, and access to international markets. Emerging economies like China and India capitalized on global trade to lift millions out of poverty, while developed nations benefited from cheaper goods and expanded consumer markets.

However, globalization also intensified economic disparities within and between nations. While multinational corporations thrived, small businesses struggled to compete in an increasingly interconnected marketplace. Manufacturing jobs in developed economies were outsourced to countries with lower labor costs, leading to deindustrialization and economic decline in regions dependent on traditional industries. For workers, globalization often meant increased precarity, stagnant wages, and weakened bargaining power.

The rise of global supply chains further entrenched inequalities. Companies like Nike and Apple outsourced production to developing nations, where lax labor regulations and lower wages enabled cost reductions. While these practices increased corporate profits and consumer affordability, they often relied on exploitative labor conditions. In regions like Southeast Asia, garment workers endured grueling hours and unsafe factories, echoing the labor struggles of the Gilded Age.

The interconnectedness fostered by globalization also enabled the rapid consolidation of technological power. Multinational tech companies such as Amazon, Google, and Facebook emerged as dominant forces, leveraging global markets to achieve unprecedented scale. These companies, benefiting from deregulated markets, data monopolization, and cross-border operations, now mirror the monopolistic tendencies of the industrial giants of the past.

The Winners and Losers of the Global Economy

The combination of neoliberalism and globalization produced clear winners and losers. For the global elite—corporate executives, investors, and knowledge-based professionals—the era brought unprecedented wealth and opportunity. The financialization of the economy, driven by deregulation and technological innovation, created vast fortunes in banking, investment, and tech industries. Cities like New York, London, and Hong Kong became global financial hubs, attracting capital and talent from around the world.

Meanwhile, working-class communities in developed nations faced economic dislocation and declining prospects. The loss of manufacturing jobs in places like the American Midwest and Northern England devastated local economies, leading to rising unemployment, poverty, and social unrest. In developing nations, the benefits of globalization were unevenly distributed. While urban centers experienced rapid growth, rural areas often remained mired in poverty, excluded from the gains of global commerce.

Neoliberalism's Legacy and Its Critics

By the early 21st century, the limitations and consequences of neoliberalism had become increasingly apparent. The 2008 global financial crisis exposed the fragility of deregulated markets, as reckless financial practices led to widespread economic collapse. Governments intervened with massive bailouts and stimulus measures, underscoring the need for regulatory oversight in a system that had prioritized profit over stability.

Critics of neoliberalism argue that its emphasis on free markets and privatization has deepened inequality, eroded social safety nets, and weakened democratic governance. Figures like economist Thomas Piketty have highlighted the concentration of wealth among the global elite, warning that unchecked capitalism threatens economic and social cohesion. The backlash against neoliberalism has fueled populist movements across the political spectrum, as communities left behind by globalization demand policies that address inequality and restore economic security.

The Path Forward: Balancing Growth and Equity

As we confront the legacy of neoliberalism and globalization, the central challenge remains: How can we harness the benefits of interconnected markets while addressing their inequities? The lessons of the Gilded Age and Progressive Era remind us that unregulated capitalism tends toward consolidation and exploitation, but thoughtful intervention can restore balance.

Reimagining competition in a globalized world requires policies that promote fair trade, protect workers, and ensure that economic growth benefits all members of society. Strengthening labor protections, reforming tax systems, and investing in public infrastructure are essential steps toward creating an economy that prioritizes equity alongside innovation.

Globalization is not inherently destructive, but its outcomes depend on the rules we establish to govern it. By learning from past mistakes and embracing policies that balance growth with fairness, we can chart a path toward a more inclusive and sustainable global economy—one that serves not only the interests of the powerful but the aspirations of all.

As neoliberalism's grip begins to weaken, a new challenge emerges: the dominance of technological monopolies. The deregulated, interconnected markets of the neoliberal era laid the foundation for a new wave of economic dominance: technological giants. Companies like Amazon, Google, and Facebook have reshaped commerce, data, and competition, posing questions eerily similar to those faced during the rise of industrial monopolies. The next chapter examines how the Age of Big Tech parallels and departs from earlier eras, and what it reveals about the future of capitalism.

Chapter 5: The Age of Big Tech

The early 21st century ushered in a new era of economic dominance, one defined not by steel, oil, or railroads, but by data, platforms, and digital ecosystems. The rise of Big Tech—a handful of corporations like Amazon, Google, Facebook (Meta), Apple, and Microsoft—has reshaped global markets, economies, and even societies at an unprecedented scale. Global markets enabled by neoliberal reforms became fertile ground for the rapid ascent of Big Tech, where deregulated innovation converged with the unprecedented value of data. Much like the industrial monopolies of the Gilded Age, today's tech giants have consolidated immense power, leveraging technological innovation, market efficiencies, and data collection to dominate entire industries. Yet, in the process, they have revived old questions about competition, labor, and governance, raising concerns about fairness, accountability, and the future of capitalism itself.

This chapter explores the rise of Big Tech, examining the parallels and divergences between the technological monopolies of today and the industrial titans of the past. We analyze how these companies amassed their power, the consequences for workers and consumers, and the regulatory challenges they present. As with the Gilded Age, the central dilemma persists: Can innovation and competition coexist, or does the relentless pursuit of efficiency inevitably lead to consolidation and exploitation?

The Rise of the Tech Giants

The origins of Big Tech can be traced to the late 20th century, as advances in computing, the internet, and software revolutionized communication, commerce, and information. Companies like Microsoft and Apple emerged as early pioneers, creating the hardware and operating systems that laid the foundation for the digital age. The launch of the World Wide Web in the 1990s further transformed the landscape, enabling new forms of connectivity and economic opportunity.

The 2000s marked a turning point. Companies such as Google, Amazon, and Facebook capitalized on the internet's rapid expansion, developing business models that disrupted traditional markets and created entirely new industries. Google revolutionized search and online advertising, becoming the gatekeeper to the world's information. Amazon redefined commerce through its e-commerce platform, logistics networks, and cloud computing services. Facebook created a social media empire, connecting billions of users while monetizing their data for targeted advertising.

These companies grew at extraordinary speeds, fueled by network effects—a phenomenon in which the value of a product or service increases as more people use it. Amazon's vast marketplace attracted sellers and buyers, creating a self-reinforcing cycle of growth. Google's dominance in search enabled it to capture more data, improving its algorithms and solidifying its position. Facebook's platforms became indispensable for communication, making it nearly impossible for competitors to challenge its scale.

The result has been the concentration of economic and technological power in the hands of a few companies. Today, these firms control vast portions of digital infrastructure, from online marketplaces and advertising networks to cloud computing and app ecosystems. Their influence extends beyond commerce and into areas like media, education, healthcare, and even politics, as the platforms they control shape public discourse and access to information.

Parallels to the Gilded Age Monopolies

The rise of Big Tech bears striking similarities to the industrial monopolies of the Gilded Age. Like Rockefeller's Standard Oil, Big

Tech companies have achieved dominance through vertical and horizontal integration. Amazon controls not only its e-commerce platform but also its logistics, warehousing, and delivery networks, creating efficiencies that few competitors can match. Similarly, Apple controls both its hardware and software ecosystems, locking users into a seamless but closed environment.

The exploitation of data as a resource mirrors the industrial monopolies' use of oil, steel, and railroads to achieve market dominance. Data—collected from users, businesses, and governments—has become the most valuable commodity of the digital age. Tech giants leverage this data to refine their algorithms, target consumers with precision, and expand their influence into new markets. As Standard Oil once controlled the flow of oil, companies like Google and Facebook now control the flow of information, raising concerns about transparency, bias, and manipulation.

The labor dynamics of Big Tech also echo those of the industrial era. While tech companies present themselves as innovators and disruptors, their success often relies on precarious labor. For instance, an Amazon warehouse worker might process hundreds of packages per hour under tight surveillance, with quotas so demanding that some skip breaks to keep up. Gig economy platforms like Uber and DoorDash promise flexibility but leave workers without benefits, protections, or collective bargaining power. Meanwhile, the tech industry's white-collar workers, though well-compensated, often face intense pressure to deliver innovation under demanding deadlines.

The Consequences of Tech Monopolies

The dominance of Big Tech has produced profound consequences for economies, workers, and consumers. While these companies have driven innovation, created new industries, and lowered costs for consumers, their consolidation of power has come at a significant price.

1. **Market Control and Competition**: Tech monopolies stifle competition by acquiring potential rivals, leveraging their vast resources to undercut competitors, and creating barriers to entry. Facebook's acquisitions of Instagram and WhatsApp, for example, eliminated competition in social media, while

Amazon's dominance in e-commerce has marginalized smaller retailers and startups.

2. **Data Privacy and Surveillance**: The collection and monetization of personal data raise serious concerns about privacy and surveillance. Users often lack control over how their data is used, while governments and corporations exploit this information for their own ends. Scandals like Facebook's Cambridge Analytica debacle highlight the risks of unchecked data practices.

3. **Labor Exploitation**: The gig economy and warehouse labor models reflect a shift toward precarious, underregulated employment. Workers face low wages, unsafe conditions, and minimal job security, exacerbating income inequality and economic insecurity.

4. **Impact on Public Discourse**: Social media platforms, while facilitating communication, have also amplified misinformation, polarization, and manipulation. The algorithms that drive engagement often prioritize sensational content, undermining public trust and democratic processes.

Regulating Big Tech: Challenges and Opportunities

Efforts to regulate Big Tech face significant challenges. Unlike the industrial monopolies of the past, tech giants operate in global, digital markets that transcend traditional regulatory frameworks. Their complex business models—spanning e-commerce, advertising, cloud computing, and artificial intelligence—make it difficult to apply existing antitrust laws.

However, calls for regulation are growing louder. Governments around the world are exploring policies to curb Big Tech's power, including antitrust lawsuits, data privacy laws, and proposals to break up dominant firms. The European Union has taken the lead with initiatives like the General Data Protection Regulation (GDPR) and the Digital Markets Act, which aim to protect user privacy and ensure fair competition. In the United States, bipartisan support for antitrust action is building, with lawmakers targeting companies like Amazon, Google, and Facebook for their anti-competitive practices.

The challenge lies in balancing regulation with innovation. While it is essential to curb the excesses of tech monopolies, policymakers must ensure that regulation does not stifle technological progress or limit the benefits of digital platforms. Striking this balance will require creative solutions that address the unique nature of the digital economy while fostering competition, protecting workers, and safeguarding democratic institutions.

The Future of Innovation and Competition

The Age of Big Tech has redefined the boundaries of economic power, innovation, and competition. Like the industrial monopolies of the Gilded Age, today's tech giants have reshaped markets and created immense wealth, but their dominance has come at the cost of competition, labor security, and democratic accountability. The central challenge of our time is to address these consequences without stifling the innovation that drives progress.

The lessons of the past remind us that unregulated capitalism tends toward consolidation and exploitation. Just as the Progressive Era and New Deal brought reforms to balance growth with fairness, the digital age demands new policies to govern technological monopolies. By reimagining regulation, protecting workers, and ensuring that innovation benefits society as a whole, we can create a more equitable and competitive future—one where technology serves humanity, rather than the other way around.

As technology reshapes markets, it also transforms the nature of work itself. Can we address the precarity of labor in a digital economy, or will innovation continue to come at the cost of workers? The next chapter explores the shifting dynamics of labor in the gig economy, where flexibility, exploitation, and economic insecurity collide.

Chapter 6: Labor in the Gig Economy

The emergence of the gig economy represents one of the most profound transformations in the labor market of the 21st century. Enabled by digital platforms, flexible work arrangements, and an increasingly globalized workforce, the gig economy promises freedom and opportunity for millions. Companies like Uber, Lyft, DoorDash, and Instacart have redefined employment models, replacing traditional jobs with on-demand, task-based labor. On the surface, the gig economy appears to offer workers autonomy, flexibility, and entrepreneurial independence. However, beneath this veneer lies a stark reality: precarious employment, minimal protections, and growing economic insecurity.

The gig economy reflects both the promise and peril of technological innovation. It mirrors earlier periods of labor disruption, from the industrial revolution to the rise of service-based economies but amplifies these trends through digital platforms and algorithmic management. This chapter explores the origins, dynamics, and consequences of the gig economy, examining its impact on workers, businesses, and society. By analyzing the forces that drive this shift, we can better understand how labor markets must adapt to ensure equity, security, and sustainability in a digital age.

The Origins of the Gig Economy

The gig economy emerged at the intersection of technological innovation, economic necessity, and shifting cultural attitudes toward work. In the wake of the 2008 global financial crisis, millions of workers faced unemployment, stagnant wages, and limited opportunities for stable employment. At the same time, advances in digital technology—particularly the proliferation of smartphones, GPS, and mobile applications—enabled new platforms to connect workers with short-term, on-demand jobs.

Companies like Uber and TaskRabbit pioneered this model, presenting it as a win-win solution for both workers and consumers. Workers could earn income on their own schedules, while consumers gained access to affordable, convenient services. This model quickly expanded to encompass a wide range of industries, including transportation, food delivery, home services, and freelance work. The rapid growth of platforms like Airbnb, Upwork, and Fiverr further demonstrated the scalability and profitability of gig-based labor.

Underlying the gig economy is the shift from traditional employment to independent contracting. Gig workers are classified as independent contractors rather than employees, which allows companies to avoid providing benefits such as health insurance, paid leave, and retirement plans. While this classification reduces costs for businesses, it also places the burden of economic risk squarely on the shoulders of workers.

The Gig Worker Experience: Flexibility and Precarity

At the heart of the gig economy lies a paradox: the same flexibility that attracts workers to gig jobs also contributes to their economic vulnerability. Gig work is often presented as a choice—a way for individuals to control their schedules, pursue multiple income streams, or supplement their primary earnings. For some, particularly those with access to other resources or stable employment, gig work offers meaningful autonomy.

However, for many gig workers, flexibility is a necessity rather than a choice. Economic hardship, lack of alternatives, and structural inequalities drive individuals into gig jobs where they face significant precarity. Key aspects of the gig worker experience include:

- **Unstable Income**: Gig workers are paid per task or project, leaving their earnings unpredictable and inconsistent. Fluctuating demand, platform fees, and competition among workers further erode take-home pay.
- **Lack of Benefits**: As independent contractors, gig workers are excluded from traditional employment benefits, such as health

insurance, sick leave, and retirement contributions. This absence of a safety net leaves workers vulnerable to financial shocks and long-term insecurity.

- **Algorithmic Management**: Digital platforms use algorithms to assign tasks, monitor performance, and determine pay. While these systems optimize efficiency, they also subject workers to opaque, impersonal management practices that can be exploitative and dehumanizing.

- **Exploitation of Vulnerable Workers**: Immigrants, women, and low-income individuals are disproportionately represented in gig work, often because of barriers to traditional employment. This dynamic exacerbates existing inequalities and reinforces cycles of economic insecurity.

Studies have shown that gig workers frequently earn below minimum wage when accounting for expenses such as vehicle maintenance, fuel, and platform fees. A 2020 report by the Economic Policy Institute found that Uber drivers in the United States earned an average of $9.21 per hour after expenses—well below the federal minimum wage in many states.

The Business of Gig Work: Platforms and Profitability

The gig economy thrives on the profitability of platforms that act as intermediaries between workers and consumers. These platforms rely on a combination of technological innovation, market efficiencies, and minimal labor costs to achieve dominance. Key elements of the gig economy business model include:

- **Scalability**: Digital platforms can scale rapidly, connecting millions of workers and consumers across geographies. This scalability allows platforms to dominate markets and achieve near-monopoly status.

- **Cost Externalization**: By classifying workers as independent contractors, gig platforms avoid the costs associated with employment, such as benefits, insurance, and payroll taxes. This cost-saving measure enhances profitability but shifts economic risks onto workers.

- **Dynamic Pricing and Competition**: Platforms use algorithms to implement dynamic pricing, adjusting rates based on demand, competition, and worker availability. While this benefits consumers and platform profits, it often undermines worker earnings.

- **Data Exploitation**: Gig platforms collect vast amounts of data on workers, customers, and markets. This data is used to optimize operations, predict demand, and maintain competitive advantages, mirroring Big Tech's reliance on data as a resource.

The success of platforms like Uber and DoorDash demonstrates the profitability of gig-based models, but their dominance raises questions about fairness, sustainability, and accountability. The absence of regulation has allowed gig companies to prioritize shareholder returns while sidestepping responsibilities to workers and society.

Labor Rights and the Fight for Protections
The rise of the gig economy has sparked a global debate about labor rights, worker classification, and the future of employment. As gig work becomes increasingly prevalent, policymakers, labor advocates, and workers themselves are challenging the status quo and demanding reforms. Key areas of focus include:

- **Worker Classification**: The classification of gig workers as independent contractors lies at the heart of the debate. Labor advocates argue that gig workers function as employees and should receive corresponding protections and benefits. Legal battles, such as California's Proposition 22, highlight the contentious nature of this issue.

- **Minimum Wage and Benefits**: Efforts to establish minimum wage guarantees, paid leave, and health insurance for gig workers have gained traction in various jurisdictions. For example, New York City implemented a minimum pay rate for ride-share drivers to ensure fair compensation.

- **Collective Bargaining**: Gig workers lack the right to unionize or collectively bargain under current labor laws. However, emerging worker organizations and coalitions are mobilizing to advocate for better conditions and protections.

- **Regulatory Oversight**: Policymakers are exploring regulations to hold gig platforms accountable for worker treatment, safety standards, and transparency in algorithmic management. The European Union and countries like Canada are leading efforts to establish clearer rules for gig work.

The fight for labor rights in the gig economy echoes earlier struggles for worker protections during the industrial revolution and the Progressive Era. Just as those movements reshaped labor markets to address exploitation, today's reforms aim to balance flexibility with fairness.

Rethinking Work in a Digital Age

The gig economy exemplifies the contradictions of modern capitalism—offering innovation, convenience, and flexibility while exacerbating inequality, exploitation, and insecurity. As the gig economy continues to expand, it raises fundamental questions about the nature of work, the role of employers, and the responsibilities of governments in protecting workers.

Ensuring a fairer gig economy requires bold reforms that prioritize worker protections, establish minimum standards, and hold platforms accountable for their impact. By rethinking labor laws, encouraging collective bargaining, and addressing systemic inequalities, we can create a future of work that balances flexibility with security.

The next chapter explores the broader implications of these dynamics, examining how worker-centric economic models can reimagine competition, equity, and progress in an increasingly digital world.

Chapter 7:
Comparative Antitrust Approaches

As monopolistic dominance reemerges in the digital age, the question of how to regulate and restrain corporate power has taken center stage in global economic policy. Governments across the world are grappling with how to address the immense influence of Big Tech and other market-dominating entities, drawing on historical antitrust principles while adapting to the challenges of modern economies.

The approaches taken to antitrust enforcement, however, are far from uniform. This chapter examines the strategies employed by the United States, the European Union, and China, highlighting their unique philosophies, policies, and impacts on global markets. While the United States relies on its historical legacy of antitrust regulation shaped during the Progressive Era, the European Union has pioneered a more proactive and expansive regulatory approach. Other nations, including China, India, and Australia, are also experimenting with policies that reflect their unique economic, cultural, and political priorities.

This chapter explores these comparative antitrust approaches, examining their historical roots, philosophical underpinnings, and practical applications. By analyzing the strengths and shortcomings of each model, we gain critical insights into how global antitrust regulation can evolve to meet the challenges of 21st-century capitalism.

The American Approach: A Legacy of Antitrust Principles

The roots of U.S. antitrust regulation lie in the Gilded Age and the Progressive Era, when industrial monopolies threatened competition, workers' rights, and economic democracy. Laws such as the Sherman Antitrust Act (1890) and the Clayton Antitrust Act (1914) emerged in response to corporate titans like Standard Oil and U.S. Steel, establishing legal frameworks to break up monopolies and prevent anti-competitive practices.

In the mid-20th century, the U.S. government actively enforced these laws to dismantle monopolies and protect markets. Landmark cases, such as the breakup of AT&T in 1984, demonstrated the federal government's commitment to ensuring fair competition. However, beginning in the 1980s, a shift in economic philosophy—driven by the Chicago School of Economics—emphasized consumer welfare as the primary focus of antitrust enforcement. Under this framework, monopolistic power was tolerated as long as it resulted in lower prices or greater efficiencies for consumers.

This narrow interpretation of antitrust law has allowed Big Tech companies to consolidate power largely unchecked. For example, Facebook's acquisition of Instagram in 2012 and WhatsApp in 2014 faced little regulatory resistance, enabling the company to eliminate competition and secure its dominance in the social media market. Companies like Amazon, Google, and Facebook argue that their dominance benefits consumers through lower costs, greater convenience, and improved services. Critics, however, contend that the consumer welfare standard fails to account for broader economic and social harms, such as the suppression of competition, the exploitation of workers, and the erosion of democratic institutions.

Recent developments signal a potential shift in U.S. antitrust policy. High-profile lawsuits against Google, Amazon, and Facebook reflect growing bipartisan support for stronger enforcement. Congressional investigations, spearheaded by figures like Senator Elizabeth Warren and Representative David Cicilline, have called for the breakup of Big Tech and a return to the principles of structural regulation. The Federal Trade Commission (FTC) and the Department of Justice (DOJ) are increasingly focused on revisiting mergers, acquisitions, and monopolistic practices that have gone unchallenged for decades.

The European Approach: Proactive Regulation and Consumer Protection

In contrast to the United States, the European Union (EU) has adopted a more interventionist and proactive approach to antitrust enforcement. The EU's competition policy, rooted in the Treaty of Rome (1957) and overseen by the European Commission, prioritizes not only consumer welfare but also market fairness, innovation, and economic diversity.

A key difference between the American and European models lies in enforcement philosophy. While the U.S. focuses on preventing consumer harm, the EU seeks to prevent the abuse of dominant positions and ensure a level playing field for competitors. This broader mandate has enabled the EU to take decisive action against Big Tech, holding companies accountable for anti-competitive behavior, data exploitation, and privacy violations.

- **Google**: The European Commission has fined Google over $9 billion in a series of antitrust cases:
- **Search Engine Dominance**: Google was penalized for prioritizing its own services in search results, limiting competition in digital markets.
- **Android Operating System**: The Commission found Google guilty of restricting smartphone manufacturers from using alternative operating systems.
- **Digital Advertising Practices**: Google's dominance in online advertising was criticized for preventing rivals from gaining market share and stifling innovation.
- **Apple**: The EU has investigated Apple's App Store practices, focusing on the company's control over app distribution and its imposition of fees on developers.
- **Amazon**: The Commission has accused Amazon of abusing its marketplace dominance by using third-party seller data to prioritize its own products.

The General Data Protection Regulation (GDPR), introduced in 2018, further highlights the EU's commitment to protecting consumer rights and regulating corporate behavior. GDPR established strict guidelines for data privacy, giving users greater control over their personal information and imposing significant penalties on companies that violate these standards. This regulatory model serves as a benchmark for other nations grappling with similar issues.

While the EU's approach has been praised for its assertiveness and consumer focus, critics argue that it risks stifling innovation and placing undue burdens on businesses. However, the EU's success in challenging Big Tech demonstrates the potential of proactive regulation to address modern monopolistic practices.

China's Approach: Centralized Control and State Priorities

China's approach to antitrust regulation reflects the unique interplay between state control and market forces. While China has embraced market liberalization and technological innovation, its regulatory policies are deeply shaped by the priorities of the central government. Antitrust enforcement in China serves both economic and political objectives, ensuring market stability while reinforcing state authority. This dual approach allows for swift and decisive action against monopolistic practices but often comes at the cost of transparency and fairness. Regulatory decisions can align with broader political priorities, creating uncertainty for businesses and raising questions about the impartiality of enforcement.

In recent years, China has intensified its scrutiny of domestic tech giants such as Alibaba, Tencent, and Meituan. The government has targeted monopolistic practices, including platform exclusivity agreements, predatory pricing, and data exploitation. For example:

- **Alibaba**: In 2021, Chinese regulators fined Alibaba $2.8 billion for anti-competitive practices, accusing the company of forcing merchants to choose its platform over competitors.
- **Ant Group**: The government halted Ant Group's IPO and imposed new financial regulations to limit its dominance in digital payments and fintech.

Unlike Western models, China's regulatory approach often involves direct intervention, with the government exercising significant influence over corporate behavior. While this allows for swift enforcement, it also raises concerns about transparency, fairness, and the broader implications of state control over private enterprise.

Global Lessons and Emerging Trends

The diversity of antitrust approaches around the world offers valuable lessons for addressing modern monopolistic power:

1. **The Need for Flexibility**: Traditional antitrust laws, designed for industrial economies, must be updated to address the complexities of digital markets. Policymakers must account for

factors such as data dominance, algorithmic competition, and platform ecosystems.

2. **Balancing Innovation and Regulation**: While strong regulation is essential to curbing monopolistic abuses, it must be carefully designed to avoid stifling innovation. Policies should foster competition while encouraging technological progress.

3. **Global Cooperation**: In an interconnected digital economy, monopolistic practices often transcend borders. Greater international collaboration is needed to harmonize antitrust enforcement and address cross-border challenges. Frameworks such as the International Competition Network (ICN) and the OECD Competition Committee provide platforms for countries to share best practices, coordinate enforcement efforts, and address the challenges posed by global monopolistic power. These collaborations demonstrate that a unified approach can strengthen regulatory effectiveness without stifling innovation.

4. **Protecting Workers and Consumers**: Antitrust regulation must move beyond narrow interpretations of consumer welfare to address broader economic and social harms, including labor

exploitation, income inequality, and the erosion of democratic accountability.

Look towards a New Antitrust Framework

The comparative study of antitrust approaches reveals the challenges and opportunities of regulating monopolistic power in the digital age. While the United States grapples with the legacy of its consumer welfare standard, the European Union's proactive model demonstrates the potential of interventionist policies to safeguard competition and consumer rights. China's centralized approach, though effective, highlights the risks of overreach and state control.

The path forward requires a reimagined antitrust framework—one that balances innovation with accountability, competition with equity, and progress with fairness. By learning from global experiences, policymakers can craft solutions that address the unique challenges of modern capitalism, ensuring that markets remain dynamic, inclusive, and just. But as we look to the future, a critical question arises: What would an economy look like if workers, not just corporations, were placed at its center?

In the next chapter, we explore alternative economic models that prioritize workers, equity, and sustainability, offering a vision for how economies can evolve to better serve society in an era of technological transformation.

Chapter 8:
Worker-Centric Economic Models

In a world where economic systems are increasingly dominated by corporate power, the role and rights of workers have often been relegated to the margins of policy and discourse. The rise of monopolistic enterprises, particularly in the digital age, has not only stifled competition but also exacerbated economic inequality and eroded labor protections. As explored in the previous chapter, unchecked corporate dominance highlights the shortcomings of traditional antitrust approaches and raises the question: How can economic systems better empower workers while fostering fair competition? However, history reminds us that alternatives exist—economic models that prioritize workers as central stakeholders, fostering equitable, sustainable, and resilient economies.

This chapter explores worker-centric economic models, analyzing their origins, principles, and potential for reshaping modern economies. By drawing on successful historical examples, emerging innovations, and contemporary policy proposals, we examine how shifting focus from profit maximization to worker empowerment can create systems that are both just and economically vibrant. From cooperatives to stakeholder capitalism, these models challenge the status quo and provide a vision for economies that serve the many, not just the few.

The Rise and Legacy of Worker-Centric Models

Worker-centric economic models are not new. These approaches arose as a direct response to earlier economic systems that prioritized profit over labor, particularly during the Industrial Revolution, when workers faced widespread exploitation and inequality. Their relevance today underscores a persistent need to address similar challenges in modern capitalism. Their roots can be traced back to 19th-century labor movements and early cooperative enterprises that sought to empower workers in response to industrial exploitation.

- **The Rochdale Cooperative Movement (1844)**: Born in England during the Industrial Revolution, the Rochdale Pioneers established principles that remain foundational to cooperatives worldwide. These principles, including democratic control, shared ownership, and equitable distribution of profits, set a precedent for worker-centric models that followed. They inspired cooperative enterprises globally and laid the groundwork for contemporary innovations like worker cooperatives and platform cooperatives, where worker participation and shared governance remain central tenets. By collectively owning and operating businesses, workers and consumers shared decision-making power and economic benefits, fostering equity and local sustainability.

- **Labor Unions and the Progressive Era**: In the late 19th and early 20th centuries, labor unions played a critical role in advocating for fair wages, safe working conditions, and the eight-hour workday. These efforts not only improved workers' lives but also demonstrated the power of collective bargaining as a mechanism for economic justice.

- **Post-War Social Democracies**: In the aftermath of World War II, nations like Sweden, Germany, and Norway implemented worker-friendly policies, including codetermination laws that gave employees representation on corporate boards. These models balanced economic growth with social protections, creating some of the world's most prosperous and equitable societies.

The historical successes of worker-centric models demonstrate that economies can thrive when workers are treated as partners, not just labor inputs. While these approaches faced challenges—such as resistance from entrenched corporate interests—they provide valuable lessons for addressing the inequities of modern capitalism.

Contemporary Worker-Centric Innovations

In the 21st century, worker-centric models are experiencing a resurgence, driven by growing discontent with economic inequality, technological disruption, and the precarious nature of work. This resurgence directly challenges the monopolistic corporate practices discussed in previous chapters, offering an alternative to systems that consolidate power at the expense of workers. By prioritizing equity and shared governance, these models aim to counteract the economic and social harms created by unchecked corporate dominance. Key contemporary innovations include:

1. **Worker Cooperatives** Worker cooperatives are businesses owned and operated by their employees, who share in profits and decision-making. Unlike traditional corporate structures, where power is concentrated among shareholders and executives, cooperatives distribute control equally among workers, ensuring their voices are central to governance. Studies have shown that worker cooperatives tend to be more resilient during economic downturns compared to conventional businesses, as their democratic structure fosters collective decision-making that

prioritizes long-term stability over short-term gains. For example, during the 2008 financial crisis, worker cooperatives in Europe demonstrated higher survival rates, providing an important model for economic resilience. This unique structure prioritizes worker well-being and community development over maximizing shareholder value. Unlike traditional corporations, cooperatives prioritize the well-being of workers and communities over shareholder value.

- *Example*: Mondragón Corporation in Spain, one of the world's largest worker cooperatives, employs over 80,000 people across industries. Its democratic governance structure and profit-sharing model have created stable, resilient jobs in a competitive global economy.
- *Impact*: Studies show that worker cooperatives experience lower turnover, greater job satisfaction, and stronger community ties compared to conventional businesses.

2. **Codetermination Policies** Codetermination gives workers a voice in corporate governance by requiring employee representation on company boards. This model, prevalent in Germany, ensures that corporate decisions consider the interests of workers alongside those of shareholders.
   - *Impact*: Codetermination has been credited with reducing income inequality, fostering long-term planning, and enhancing workplace stability in Germany's economy.
3. **Employee Stock Ownership Plans (ESOPs)** ESOPs enable workers to become partial owners of the companies they work for by acquiring shares through retirement plans or profit-sharing schemes.
   - *Example*: Companies like Publix Super Markets in the United States have successfully implemented ESOPs, creating wealth for employees while maintaining competitiveness.
   - *Impact*: ESOPs have been shown to increase worker loyalty, productivity, and economic security, aligning employee and company interests.

4. **Platform Cooperatives** As a response to exploitation in the gig economy, platform cooperatives aim to reclaim worker power by developing digital platforms owned and governed by workers.
   - *Example*: Driver's Seat, a cooperative of gig drivers in the U.S., allows workers to collect and monetize their own data, challenging exploitative algorithms used by traditional ride-hailing companies.
   - *Impact*: Platform cooperatives demonstrate how technology can be harnessed to empower workers rather than marginalize them.

The Principles of Worker-Centric Models

While worker-centric models vary in form, they share core principles that distinguish them from profit-driven systems:

1. **Democratic Governance**: Workers have a voice in decision-making, ensuring that corporate policies reflect their needs and values.

2. **Equitable Distribution**: Profits are shared more fairly among stakeholders, reducing income inequality and fostering economic inclusion.
3. **Long-Term Sustainability**: Worker-centric models prioritize long-term stability over short-term gains, investing in employees, communities, and environmental responsibility.
4. **Social Responsibility**: These models emphasize ethical practices, community well-being, and the dignity of labor.

By embracing these principles, worker-centric models challenge the notion that economic efficiency requires the exploitation of labor. Instead, they demonstrate that equitable systems can be both productive and just.

Challenges and Criticisms

Despite their promise, worker-centric models face significant challenges. For instance, the Mondragón Corporation in Spain, one of the largest and most successful worker cooperatives in the world, initially struggled to secure financing and compete in global markets. To address these hurdles, Mondragón developed a unique approach that combined internal capital pooling among its member cooperatives with external partnerships, ensuring access to funding while maintaining worker ownership. It also diversified its operations across multiple industries, reducing risk and fostering economic resilience. Additionally, Mondragón established its own cooperative bank, Caja Laboral, to provide financial support for worker-led ventures. Through innovation, diversification, and strong governance, it overcame these barriers to become a global example of resilience and success, demonstrating that effective policies and structural support can enable worker-centric models to thrive even in competitive environments. This demonstrates that, with the right support and adaptation, worker-centric models can thrive even in competitive environments.

- **Scale and Competitiveness**: Critics argue that worker-owned enterprises may struggle to scale or compete in global markets dominated by profit-driven corporations.
- **Access to Capital**: Worker cooperatives and platform cooperatives often face barriers to financing, as traditional investors prioritize short-term returns.

- **Cultural Barriers**: In economies steeped in shareholder capitalism, worker-centric approaches may be viewed as impractical or ideologically driven.
- **Regulatory Hurdles**: Existing legal and tax frameworks often favor traditional corporate structures, creating disadvantages for alternative models.

Addressing these challenges requires supportive policies, innovative financing mechanisms, and cultural shifts that recognize the value of worker empowerment.

A Vision for Worker-Centric Economies

Worker-centric economic models offer a compelling alternative to systems that prioritize profits over people. By addressing the structural inequalities that perpetuate economic disparity, these models not only challenge entrenched corporate dominance but also provide a framework for reducing income inequality and empowering workers as active participants in economic progress. By empowering workers as key stakeholders, these models can reduce inequality, strengthen communities, and create more resilient economies.

Policymakers, businesses, and labor advocates must work together to foster an environment where worker-centric approaches can thrive. Key steps include:

- **Policy Support**: Implementing codetermination laws, expanding access to employee ownership programs, and providing incentives for cooperatives.
- **Investment in Innovation**: Supporting platform cooperatives and other worker-led initiatives that harness technology for empowerment.
- **Education and Advocacy**: Promoting awareness of worker-centric models and their benefits to challenge cultural biases against collective ownership.

By reimagining economies with workers at the center, we can build systems that are equitable, inclusive, and sustainable. The success of these models demonstrates that alternatives to extractive capitalism are not only possible but necessary for a just future. This urgency is underscored by the rising economic inequality and erosion of worker protections discussed throughout this book—failures that traditional systems have been unable to address effectively. Worker-centric models offer a tangible path forward, proving that economic progress does not have to come at the cost of equity and dignity.

In the final chapter, we explore how these principles can inform a broader reimagining of competition, innovation, and economic governance in the 21st century.

Chapter 9:
Reimagining Competition

The modern economy stands at a crossroads. On one path lies continued consolidation, where monopolistic corporations dominate markets, exploit workers, and concentrate wealth in fewer hands. As highlighted in earlier chapters, examples like Amazon's dominance in e-commerce, Facebook's acquisitions of Instagram and WhatsApp, and the unchecked power of gig platforms reveal how traditional competition frameworks have allowed corporate power to expand at the expense of workers and consumers alike. On the other lies an alternative vision—one where competition fosters innovation, equity, and shared prosperity. To move forward, we must fundamentally rethink what competition means, who it serves, and how it can be structured to build economies that benefit everyone.

This chapter explores how competition can be reimagined to address the failures of extractive capitalism, from rising inequality to the erosion of labor protections. Drawing from history, contemporary policy proposals, and emerging innovations, we examine strategies that promote fair competition, empower workers, and ensure sustainable progress. By rebalancing power dynamics and placing people at the center of economic systems, we can chart a path toward economies that reward innovation without sacrificing equity.

The Shortcomings of Traditional Competition

Competition is often hailed as the engine of capitalism, driving innovation, lowering prices, and improving consumer choice. While this traditional view has yielded significant benefits, it requires reform to ensure fairness, inclusivity, and sustainability in an increasingly complex and consolidated global economy. However, in practice, traditional interpretations of competition have led to outcomes that undermine its intended benefits.

1. **Market Concentration**: The rise of monopolies and oligopolies, particularly in the digital age, has stifled competition rather than encouraging it. Companies like Amazon, Google, and Facebook have leveraged their scale to eliminate rivals, resulting in market dominance that limits consumer choice and suppresses innovation.

2. **Labor Exploitation**: Traditional competition often prioritizes cost-cutting over worker well-being. The gig economy, as explored in previous chapters, exemplifies this dynamic, where corporations exploit labor flexibility to minimize wages and benefits.

3. **Short-Termism**: Competition that focuses solely on shareholder value encourages short-term gains at the expense of long-term sustainability. Companies under pressure to deliver quarterly profits often neglect investments in workers, communities, and innovation.

4. **Global Inequality**: Unchecked global competition has exacerbated economic disparities, particularly in developing nations, where labor and environmental standards are often sacrificed to attract investment and production.

These shortcomings reveal a fundamental flaw in how competition is defined and regulated—a flaw rooted in outdated policies, inadequate enforcement, and corporate behaviors that prioritize consolidation over fair market dynamics. Rather than fostering dynamic, inclusive economies, traditional competition has concentrated power, widened inequality, and undermined the dignity of labor.

Principles for Reimagining Competition

To create a fairer and more sustainable economy, we must redefine competition based on principles that balance innovation, equity, and accountability. These principles include:

1. **Leveling the Playing Field**: Markets must be structured to ensure that businesses of all sizes can compete fairly. This requires stronger antitrust enforcement, policies to prevent monopolistic practices, and support for small businesses and cooperatives.

2. **Empowering Workers**: Fair competition must prioritize labor rights, ensuring that workers are treated as stakeholders rather than expendable costs. Policies like codetermination, collective bargaining, and living wage guarantees can ensure that competition does not come at the expense of workers.

3. **Fostering Innovation**: Competition should reward creativity, long-term investment, and technological progress rather than consolidation. Public investment in research, education, and infrastructure can spur innovation while creating shared benefits.

4. **Sustainability and Accountability**: True competition must consider environmental and social impacts. Companies should be held accountable for their contributions to climate change, inequality, and public well-being, ensuring that economic progress aligns with broader societal goals.

By embracing these principles, we can redefine competition as a force that drives not just economic growth, but also equity, innovation, and sustainability.

Case Studies in Fair Competition

To understand how competition can be reimagined, it is instructive to examine real-world examples where innovative policies and practices have created fairer, more inclusive markets.

1. **The European Union's Antitrust Framework** The EU's proactive approach to regulating monopolistic practices demonstrates how competition policies can promote fairness and innovation. Unlike the U.S. antitrust model, which often focuses narrowly on consumer welfare and lower prices, the EU emphasizes preventing dominance and ensuring a level playing

field for competitors. This broader mandate allows the EU to address structural imbalances in markets and promote long-term fairness. By holding companies like Google and Apple accountable for anti-competitive behavior, the EU has set global standards for market fairness and consumer protection.

- *Impact*: The EU's fines and regulatory actions have forced tech companies to alter their practices, fostering more competitive digital markets.

2. **Germany's Codetermination Policies** Germany's codetermination model, which gives workers representation on corporate boards, ensures that competition considers labor interests. This approach reduces income inequality, improves workplace stability, and fosters long-term decision-making.

- *Impact*: Codetermination has contributed to Germany's economic resilience and equitable growth, offering a model for balancing competition with worker empowerment.

3. **The Success of Platform Cooperatives** Platform cooperatives offer an alternative to exploitative gig economy platforms by

placing ownership and governance in the hands of workers. For example, Driver's Seat allows gig drivers to collectively own their data and advocate for fair wages and conditions.

- *Impact*: Platform cooperatives demonstrate how technology can be harnessed to promote fair competition and worker equity.

4. **The Scandinavian Social Market Model** Countries like Sweden and Norway combine competitive markets with strong social protections. Policies such as universal healthcare, free education, and progressive taxation ensure that economic competition serves broader societal goals.

- *Impact*: These models show that competition and equity can coexist, creating prosperous, sustainable economies.

Policy Proposals for a New Competitive Framework

Reimagining competition requires bold policy reforms that address the structural flaws of current systems. These reforms align closely with the worker-centric models discussed in Chapter 8, which emphasize equity, shared ownership, and long-term sustainability. By integrating policies that empower workers as stakeholders, such as codetermination and worker cooperatives, we can create competitive markets that prioritize innovation while ensuring fairness and inclusivity. Key proposals include:

1. **Strengthening Antitrust Enforcement** Governments must take decisive action to break up monopolies, prevent anti-competitive mergers, and hold corporations accountable for market abuses. This includes modernizing antitrust laws to address digital platforms and data-driven monopolies.

2. **Promoting Worker Ownership and Participation** Policies that encourage worker ownership, such as employee stock ownership plans (ESOPs) and cooperatives, can redistribute economic power and ensure that workers benefit from competition.

3. **Incentivizing Sustainable Business Practices** Governments can implement policies that reward companies for prioritizing sustainability, such as tax incentives for green innovation and penalties for environmental harm.

4. **Public Investment in Innovation and Infrastructure** By investing in education, research, and public infrastructure, governments can create environments where innovation thrives and benefits are widely shared. This includes funding initiatives that support small businesses and worker-led enterprises.

5. **Ensuring Global Fairness** International cooperation is essential to address global economic inequalities. Trade agreements should include labor and environmental standards to ensure fair competition across borders.

New Era of Competition

Reimagining competition is not simply an economic imperative; it is a moral one. The failures of traditional competition have concentrated power, deepened inequality, and undermined worker dignity. By redefining competition to prioritize equity, innovation, and sustainability, we can build economies that serve the many, not the few. The principles and policies explored in this chapter offer a roadmap for this transformation. From stronger antitrust enforcement to worker empowerment and sustainable practices, a reimagined competitive framework can foster dynamic, resilient, and inclusive economies. As we look to the future, the challenge lies not only in envisioning this new era of competition but in building the political will to make it a reality.

This book has explored the roots of monopolistic power, the erosion of labor protections, and the promise of alternative models. The path forward requires courage, creativity, and a commitment to equity. By embracing bold reforms and reimagining the role of workers, businesses, and governments, we can create economies that reflect our shared values and aspirations—economies where competition drives progress for all.

Conclusion: A Vision for Equitable and Sustainable Competition

As we stand at the precipice of a new economic era, the lessons of history, the realities of the present, and the aspirations for the future converge to offer us a clear choice: continue down the path of consolidation, inequality, and exploitation, or embrace bold reforms that prioritize equity, sustainability, and shared prosperity. This book has explored the roots of monopolistic power, the erosion of worker protections, and the transformative potential of worker-centric models. Now, as we look forward, it is clear that reimagining competition is both a necessity and an opportunity to build economies that reflect our shared values.

The failures of traditional competition—rising inequality, suppressed innovation, labor exploitation, and environmental harm—are not inevitable. They are challenges we have the power to overcome. By choosing bold reforms and a vision grounded in fairness and equity, we can reclaim competition as a tool to unlock human potential and build a future defined by shared prosperity. By embracing an alternative vision, we can reclaim competition as a force for progress, not just for profits.

Revisiting the Core Themes

Throughout this book, we have identified the structural flaws of modern capitalism and proposed pathways for transformation:

1. **The Return of Monopolistic Power**: The rise of Big Tech and corporate consolidation has mirrored the monopolies of the Gilded Age. Companies have leveraged their dominance to suppress competition, exploit workers, and centralize wealth, revealing the urgent need for stronger antitrust enforcement and innovative regulatory frameworks.

2. **The Erosion of Labor Protections**: From the gig economy to digital platforms, modern capitalism has devalued labor, creating precarious conditions for workers. We explored worker-centric models, such as cooperatives, codetermination, and employee ownership, as pathways to empower workers and ensure they share in economic progress.

3. **Reimagining Competition**: The traditional view of competition—focused narrowly on consumer welfare and short-term profits—must evolve. A new framework for competition

prioritizes fairness, labor rights, innovation, and sustainability, ensuring that markets serve broader societal goals.

These themes offer more than a critique; they provide a foundation for actionable change. By addressing the root causes of inequality and rebalancing power dynamics, we can design systems that are both just and resilient.

A Call for Bold Reforms

The reforms outlined throughout this book are not incremental adjustments; they are bold and transformative steps toward a fairer economic system. Key proposals include:

- **Strengthening Antitrust Enforcement**: Modernizing antitrust laws to address digital monopolies, prevent anti-competitive mergers, and dismantle concentrated corporate power.
- **Empowering Workers**: Encouraging worker ownership, codetermination, and collective bargaining to ensure workers have a voice in economic decisions and share in prosperity.

- **Investing in Innovation and Sustainability**: Public investment in education, infrastructure, and green technologies to drive inclusive, long-term progress.

- **Ensuring Global Fairness**: International cooperation to harmonize labor, environmental, and trade standards, preventing a race to the bottom in global markets.

These reforms are ambitious, but they are grounded in both historical precedent and contemporary success stories. From Germany's codetermination policies to the resilience of worker cooperatives like Mondragón, we have seen that alternatives are not only possible but proven.

The Role of Governments, Businesses, and Workers

Achieving this vision requires a shared commitment from all stakeholders in society:

- **Governments** must take the lead in implementing regulatory reforms, investing in public goods, and ensuring that markets operate fairly and transparently.
- **Businesses** must recognize their responsibility to stakeholders beyond shareholders—including workers, communities, and the environment.
- **Workers and Civil Society** must continue to advocate for their rights, organize for collective power, and demand systems that reflect their needs and aspirations.

The path forward is not the responsibility of any single entity but a collective effort to redefine the purpose and structure of our economic systems.

A Future Worth Building

At its core, this book has argued that economies must serve people, not the other way around. This is a vision of hope—a belief that economic systems can be harnessed to uplift individuals, empower workers, and create opportunities for all. A future defined by equitable competition is one where:

- Innovation thrives, driven by creativity rather than consolidation.
- Workers are empowered as partners in economic progress, not sidelined as expendable inputs.
- Wealth is distributed more fairly, fostering stronger, more resilient communities.
- Sustainability is prioritized, ensuring that economic progress does not come at the cost of environmental and social well-being.

Reimagining competition is not a rejection of capitalism, but a redefinition of its goals and values. It is a call to reclaim the promise of economic systems that reward hard work, ingenuity, and fairness. The failures of the past need not define our future.

History has shown us that transformative change is possible when societies rise to meet their challenges with courage and creativity. The reforms we propose—bold though they may seem—are the natural next steps in an ongoing struggle for economic justice and shared prosperity.

Closing Reflection

We began this journey by examining the monopolistic forces that have shaped our economy, the erosion of competition, and the precarity faced by workers in the digital age. Along the way, we explored the principles of worker-centric models, sustainable innovation, and fair competition as pathways toward a more just future. Now, as we conclude, one truth becomes clear: the economy is not an immutable force but a human construct—one we have the power to reshape.

The choice before us is profound yet simple. We can allow systems to remain as they are, or we can embrace the opportunity to create economies that are dynamic, inclusive, and compassionate. Reimagining competition as a force that serves us all is more than a possibility—it is a promise of a brighter, fairer future. By embracing bold reforms, fostering worker empowerment, and demanding accountability from corporations and governments alike, we can build economies that reflect our shared values and aspirations.

This vision is not a distant dream; it is a beacon of hope, grounded in the belief that change is possible. Together, with courage, creativity, and collective action, we can build economies that reflect our deepest values—where opportunity flourishes, sustainability thrives, and shared prosperity becomes a reality for all.

This book is part of a larger conversation. I encourage you to reach out, share your thoughts, and engage in building the future we all deserve. The real work begins here—let's shape it together.

www.ingramcontent.com/pod-product-compliance
Lightning Source LLC
Chambersburg PA
CBHW071652240526
45469CB00021B/2219